THE NATIONAL BESTSELLERS

SOUMYA RANJAN

ISBN 978-93-5458-538-8
© SOUMYA RANJAN 2021
Published in India 2021 by Pencil

A brand of

One Point Six Technologies Pvt. Ltd.
123, Building J2, Shram Seva Premises,
Wadala Truck Terminal, Wadala (E)
Mumbai 400037, Maharashtra, INDIA
E connect@thepencilapp.com
W www.thepencilapp.com

DISCLAIMER: *The opinions expressed in this book are those of the authors and do not purport to reflect the views of the Publisher.*

Author biography

Soumya Ranjan is an English Author and one of the youngestauthor of India. He is a storyteller, influencer, motivational speaker , video creator and a fascinating designer. He has written approx. 50 poems. He is also the founder of NGO- MISSION शुरूकरें.

He also loves to read books and compile stories. He is also a comedian and a mimicry artist. He belongs to the city of Jamshedpur. He is also an animal lover and make YouTube videos which are recommended as funny.

He is also a blogger(http://soumyatalks123.blogspot.com/2021/06/what-motivates-you-to-work.html)

At a very young age he owns his studio HNS Soumya Studio

He is very humble towards animals and also he loves to help people..

He was nominated for young achievers award in Pune and his books are appreciated by many national best selling writers and also by some Bollywood actors.

He has been giving many interviews and also invited to give a Ted Talk.

He is also a motivational speaker and has been helping

many helpless people all around India.

Which are based on children fiction? This is his second novel which he has presented the love and content of suicide with a twist. He studies in Vidya Bharati Chinmaya Vidyalaya which is one of the popular schools in Telco.

He has edited many videos and has designed over 100+ posters.

You can connect with him:

joinauthorsoumya@gmail.com

Connect with Soumya via:

Instagram@its__real__soumyaranjan

Twitter @SoumyaRs91161328

Please subscribe his YouTube channel - Soumya Ranjan Author

CONTENTS

Acknowledgements

A lot of changes happened in this world due to the widespread pandemic. I also lost my mentors and , supporters. But keeping hope and facing problems and resolving them is the best way to affray with this pandemic.

Great thanks to the authors who agreed for the book.
You left YouTube, Instagram, Facebook or whatever exciting stuff we have on our phones and picked up a book.

It is never just my book . It belongs to lot of people who helped me through the process . My readers and well-wishers who support me despite the digital invasion. I am fortunate to have so many leaders to shower me with love and encourage me to do better. I would also like to thank the online delivery boys and girls who put the book on my Reader's hands. Thank you for your hard work.

I would be always be thankful to my friends, families and relatives

I am grateful to you Dixitadidi , Prernadidi , Priya didi and also to my friends .

I would like to thank Smriti - my sister, though she never supported me or encouraged me but she always gave me ideas to cope up.

I am also thankful to people who saw me growing, offered comments, motivated and encouraged towards moving further.Thank youVarunOjha for helping me throughout this.
A big thanks to my social media followers,who love me and those who don't, everyone contribute in their own way.

Life Never Goes as planned neither do what we think.
A big hug to my parents and my Mentors and all my dealers. Life wouldn't have been same without you all.

Introduction

Throughout my writing journey i have been through many exciting and amazing peoples.....

I get inspired from every people i meet as i get to learn something from them or from their life journey...

As being an author i have completed my two years of writing journey. I never tried to gain money as usual i always tried to gain crores of heart...

I used to motivate and encourage people all around the world through my posts and videos...

I never knew how i will gain success but as the time passed i started learning and started gaining knowledge and now i am what today is because of u...as there is a saying in Hindi that we should always begin with a small work to achieve something big...

If you are willing to write a story or you are willing to write a book so there is nothing such difficult to write and publish (You can check out my YouTube videos where each and every information is provided.)Always try to write something good, unique and attractive that readers should read and like it ...though i have been a struggling writer but my confidence , idea and spirit made my carrier and my journey much stronger.....

I get many messages in aday and people message me from one hope that i will help them or suggest them some solution...i never had a bad attitude and i always like to help people and solve their problem....

I am writing my first non-fiction book on the national bestsellers of India. These authors also had some experience and struggle which they shared with me to pen it down in my book. Read about their stardom and also about their journey....

In this covid pandemic we all are socially apart but our hearts are with each other. Start giving hope to every person you meet who is frustrated or is unhappy.

There are some protocols we have to follow and we can save our lives and our family's too...There are also some positive signs of the pandemic ...

I always find an inspiration in every person i meet as i find something unique in that person and also i can learns something from them..

It is never ever easy to gain fame or be trending at once as you have to struggle the full journey and also you have to choose the right path in which you are comfortable.

One advice i would like to give that never forget the person or your guru because of whom you are at this height of success .

People call me as an author or they call me by my profession –I know that my boundaries of my imagination can run wild and yet i need to touch upon your heart from my words and that's everything that matter when i sit and start writing a book.

The artist is a receptacle for emotions that come from all over the place; art we do is always free...

I have been watching some young talents who are getting a lot of encouragement and also are getting fame; so these

young talents are getting discouraged because of the lime light.........
Every artist dips his brush in his own soul; and paints his own nature into his pictures....Keep faith on god and things will get smother soon. If you are facing any problem you can message me on joinauthorsoumya@gmail.com

Praises

Small children will really get inspired from you and you are the best inspiration for them.
- Puppindar Singh

Feeling proud to have young talents like you . May you achieve big success in your life.
- Bharti Singh (Comedian)

Extremely impressed from the work of Soumya, he describes the current youth.
-The telegraph

Age is just a number but talent is always uncountable.
-HemantSoren (CM Jharkhand)

Soumya is doing extra ordinary and a marvelous job.
I really appreciate his idea of running a NGO
-Ajitabha Bose

May God's Hand be always on you and you Shine as a

bright star.
-Vipul Goyal (Comedian)

CONTENTS

{Dedicated to the national bestsellers}
RUSKIN BOND

SUDEEP NAGARKAR

AJITABHA BOSE

ANSUMAN BHAGAT

AJAY KUMAR PANDEY

ROHIT DAWESAR

STUTI CHANGLE

ADITYA NIGHOT

HIMANSHU RAI

DEVANSHI SHARMA

RUSKIN BOND

Bond was a little boy who ate a lot of koftacurryand was used to having his way. Bond was born in 1934 and lived with his parents in Jamnnagar. Then he spends a wonderful year in Delhi with his father in 1942. He refers 1943 to be the best year of his life.

Despite his suffering and lonely childhood Bond develops

an optimistic outlook on life. He choose the path of becoming an earnest writer

A search for companionship and security, undercut by a fierce independence and a tendency for risk taking ,would inform every choice he made for rest of his life. He was a child who loved to be in his own exploring bugs and bee in the palaces royal garden. Even as a child the most interaction Bond had with his contemporaries was at parties hosted by the prince of Jamnnagar. Strangely though, none of his childhood loneliness reflects in his books, which he writes mostly for children.Bond was sent to live with his grandmother in Dehradun

At ten years old bond felt that he has lost both of his parents.As Bond grew his interest started growing towards writing and what better place to begin than England , where all his favourite writers lived.

Bond reveals that how in that country he fell madly in love with a Vietnamese girl called Vu. His love story ended with a heartbreak though when she rejected him.

Besides his dissatisfication , with the life he was living there, the heartbreak could be another reason for him to pack up his bags and head back to India in 1956 . A poor pampered child is suddenly forced to grew up: a disapproving grandma , amother who is out with another man, a strict school ......ending with parents separation . No one does wonders how often the eight year old Bond is left all alone .You can actually conjure up in your mind's eye the image of a confused child trying to make sense of a world that has suddenly gone away. Bond candidly admits that he did not try to reach out to his mother and to his stepfather and probably rebuffed their overtunes. Once he finished his schooling he bagan to look for ways to achieve his ambition of becoming a writer. Before settling down in Landour , Mussorie , though bond reconnected with his mother..... Yet he goes on to adopt a Pahadi family {that still cares for Bond}, Becoming their benefactor. But what was the reason behind bond being solitute in the hills? Bond adopted a very sweet family who cares and respect bond.

Bond also makes readers travel the familiar landscape of his popular literary works for which he was also honoured with Bharat ratna and also he is awarded with many prestigious awards .

Bond was a nature lover and gazed the mountains which are near to his house in Mussorie. I always had a dream to meet the legend Ruskin sir in his cozy and comfy house.

Ruskin Bond is a quintessential part of children's literature in India and a valuable part of school education. His contributions to children's literature have been noted. ... Bond's depiction of a world beyond the window of his room entranced me as a child, and still does.

Ruskin the name was choosen by his father for him which now known worldwide.

His first short story named "Untouchable" which he wrote just at the age of 16.He decided to live in India and be a writer of 20's.At the point when he decided to be a full time writer he moved Dehradun at the age of 30.

Amazingly Bond also worked in a film with Priyankachopra which was written by him.Bond always gave a note the aspiring writers "The more you write the better you write".

His stories and essays are used in school textbooks and so he is loved by the youth and also by the young children. He has now turned 87 and still writes amazing and impressive.

As i have been in conversation with Ruskin Bond since few months and he is man of goodness.He has been the Grandfather of the teenagers.

I love to read stories and the way he puts on the content in his books. Has been appreciated by many celebrities. Many people didn't knew that did Bond knows to talk in Hindi or not? Yes ,he can talk in Hindi and used to tell people never to forget your mother tongue. Bond spent most of his struggling childhood with dark sides. Ruskin Bond has given over thousands of interviews and has only been in television many times. He was a Jolly boy and used to fetch out food from the kitchen very smoothly. I Still Think Bond is still the cutest author and he also inspired people all across the world.

His first book was viral "Room on the Roof"as the story has an essence of happiness.

Room on the Roof is about an orphaned boy named Rusty who has no real family after his parents' death. He is very lonely and sad and even though he lives with his guardian (Mr. John Harrison), he doesn't feel at home. Rusty is going through several emotions: he is confused, obliged, helpless, lonely and sad. He is confused because he is a young boy between the age of an adult and child and doesn't know who to follow or what his future holds. He is obliged to follow the orders and rules of his guardian and dares not disobey him. He feels helpless because he knows that if he disobeys Mr. John, he will get caned. Rusty doesn't have any real friends and he is so very lonely in his guardian's house.

I like this book because it was written from a teenager's

perspective. The author was seventeen when he wrote this and the story was inspired by his own experiences when he lived in Dehra. He wrote this story because he too was feeling some of the emotions that Rusty was feeling in the story. And for that reason, he decided that he would never make any revisions so readers could understand how it feels to be seventeen.

It was a great read because it has a lot of different emotions and I like the way Ruskin Bond has written it: a simple story made into such a touching and sad book.

There were a few funny descriptions, such as when Ruskin Bond described a situation as: 'When a butterfly landed on the missionary's wife's palatial bosom….' I laughed a lot and when my mum read it, she also laughed.

After reading Room on The Roof, I am looking forward to reading a few of Ruskin Bond's other stories. I wonder why children of my generation don't read more of his books. Here are some books I am interested in reading from his collection: Panther's Moon and Other Stories, The Hidden Pool, and Rusty goes to London.

I think the author has explained an important message in this book. Rusty's guardian seems to be a little racist, who chooses to live in India but not mix with the people there. I think if people live in a country, they should mix with the people and appreciate their culture.

The lesson in this story for me is to remain open as Rusty was and to follow my instincts. If Rusty had not becomes friends with the people of the bazaar he would never have had all the wonderful experiences in the story.

Ruskin Bond reminds me of Roald Dahl because they both use interesting language and really funny phrases to describe their characters and their stories. They both write simple but wonderful stories. Even though, Roald Dahl is more fantastical and Ruskin Bond's stories feel like memoirs but presented as a story.

It is not his canvas but his words, their simplicity, depth and their meaning that made his stories seem like my own. I could have been anywhere and I would have been touched all the same. In the larger scheme of things, it is the smaller things that matter more. "Ruskin Bond's words help me find my own words.

Though his books are written for children but it can be equally enjoyed by an adult too, well that's the beauty of Ruskin Bond's writing. He makes the most ordinary things extraordinary. His intricate narration carries into a different world. A world where we can find a little of ourselves. Ruskin Bond is my favourite as he is one of the writers who refuses to be brought down by predictability. His works mainly interferes with language, style and most importantly story. Encouraging young writers to try his simple style of writing.Bond added " I have always tried to achieve a prose that I easy and conversational ."

He is considered to be an icon among the teenagers and Indian writers. The Indian Council of child education has recognised his role in the growth of children literature in India and was awarded Sahitya Academy Award in 1992. The thecosy, warm, heaven like house of Ruskin Bond was purchased in 1980

The reason behind his replacement from Delhi to Mussoorie was that he was not comfortable in writing in Delhi and while he was able to write more happy while gazing the mountains and the rusty winds. He feels better to write in the morning having a nap and feels Grumpy without any afternoon seista. Ruskin Bond wrote number of stories in the lockdown and has he is old now over but the spirit and the strategy used in writing is adorable and amazing. He wanted to become a tab dancer but he has extended his figure which he will be now rejected soon. He was the tikki eater. He also won many championships in tikki eating. He ate a Lot of alootikki when he was a teenager. He has cambrige store in his hilly mountain where there are number of books of Ruskin Bond and you can meet him there evening Saturday and ofcourse click selfies with him.

SUDEEP NAGARKAR

Rapid and sustainable growth was his true passion. Being brought up in a Brahman Marathi family he was not extensively into writing in his childhood. He usually wrote diary entries, practiced essays and casual letters. Sudeep was born in Mumbai not only to meet the film stars but also to carry on his career. He was a backbencher in his school days and was beaten and throbed by every teacher he met. He was one of those who was not a studious boy but managed to gorge his way. He being a mischievous boy became a troublesome for the teachers in school. There were competitions held to write essays of five hundred words and he would hardly come to that count of words.

Owing to he was not interested in writing. Life is what in future we never knew as a possibilities come to everyone's life . In his post class six he always had fun sitting at the back with his classmates. They offered comments and did gossips about many new upcoming movies

His class comprises of a remark Book where teacher especially wrote about the students who disturbed the teachers,offered comments and did mischief. So once Sudeep bunked his class and went with his friends. The teacher and his parents got to know about Sudeep and he was played like drum in his house and everyone gave a beat to the drum and Poor Sudeep!

This incident was noted in the remark calender and smart Sudeep before one month ending of the session he changed the calendar and escaped out of it

Sudeep was promoted to class 7 and she was now used to full pants. The most exciting session becomes class 7 as students change their dressing from half pants to full trouser. Sudeep was average students scoring among 40's . He was not so dedicated to our studies and contrived to score average marks..

One of the subject teacher of Sudeep saw a sparkling future of Sudeep in his eyes. She thought that Sudeep can do much better .Sudeep also felt that the teacher is helping him at her personal level . The teacher had the true faith and presumption on Sudeep. Sudeep went home and thought and his "Mann Ki Baat" started. He said to himself " if the teacher is trusting on me then I should also be Solemon regarding my studies this time and should work hard". There was only one month left before examination and Sudeep was now the worm of studies.

The examination day arrived and Sudeep answered the Deadly questions very well by God's grace and Sudeep'shardwork showered colours in his life. As he scored 17th among the students for the first time. There was a drastic change in the infrastructure and his studies and teachers dedication worth it. Sudeep's parents were handed over the report card and the teacher appreciated his hard work

Days passed and Sudeep was now in class 10. He was now tensed this year as he was going to appear for the board exams. He somehow managed to do well and same problem was in 12th exam.
Sudeep was now on the path of Engineering. He was not able to pursue engineering smoothly and faced many difficulties.

He was not interested in pursuing engineering and never liked the IT job. When he penned down a short story and within a short time he realised that writing is his passion and he should focus on it. I always think that if anybody wants to become a writer should they study engineering because till date I have been going through many authors who first pursued engineering and then realised that writing is their passion and they should enterprise on it. This is what happened with Sudeep .

Sudeep's friend encouraged him towards publishing his first book "few things left unsaid "and Sudeep was not known to the writers community and slowly and steadily his first book got published but still he was working in the IT company.

The audience gave a good response to the book and the book became the best selling Romance novel as it was based on a real life story.

He suffered a mental heartbroke in his life when he was 19 years old.He also told that he is too young to guide someone on romantic queries but still he tries to reply as much as he can.

He became the most heart throbbing icon among the youth. Opportunities arrives all of a sudden , just we have to grab it and this formula was applied to his life.

But also conveincing an Indian parent to take writing as a full-time career was extremely difficult. The important thing was that he believed in himself and was 100% committed towards writing as most of the authors have a optional job but Sudeep wanted only writing.

Sudeep believe that Pyar , love is all what comes naturally and being in a relationship is not anybody's fault as it always comes from within. His book "You are the password of my life" disapproves the statement that a boy and a girl cannot be a friend.

Sudeep denies this fact but from childhood we have been brought up saying these things . If a boy talks to a girl the idiotic friend will start spreading rumours and we will be the part , who will get comments about being in a relationship.
Youngsters are more attracted towards love stories and every genre has their own perspective. You're the password to my life is a book based on a true story of Sudeep cousin's life. This book is all about friendship and love and it makes you believe in it. 'We all have that one person in our lives in whose absence our life seems meaningless'. The prologue of the book covers the entire title of the book 'You're the password to my life'. It is a true story that shows us that friendship is the only 'ship' that does not sink.

It is a story about friendship, love, trust and affection. It is the tale of two friends. The story is set in Pune where two friends meet in their college days and become best friends. They are a password to each other's lives. They are of two different choices but still they have a very strong bond between themselves.

They set an example that a girl and a boy can be best friends.

The book only became bestselling if you are more in flow

and in love and you connect well with the characters. He has given many blockbuster novels since few years and became a sensation for the readers.

He Encouraged authors to write always what comes from your heart by not only using good vocabulary but also with good language. Sudeep and his novels has pictured a story that things may look bad at the start but later on his determination and dedication has happy ending and every situation has something to teach us. His writing is truly based on true friendship , trust and love in a relationship.

What is it about the popularity of his books That's The Way We Met, Few Things Left Unsaid, It Started With A Friend Request, You're Trending in My Dreams, Sorry You're Not My Type or You Are The Password To My Life that have made him a national bestseller we wonder. Is it the catchy titles, true stories that connect with everyone, or his ability to describe humour, love and affection with ease?

Sudeep replies, "My stories and characters are inspired from real life. Everyone likes how I portray my proposal scenes in my books as they can relate to them.

Sudeep while he studied engineering he made a girlfriend Jasmine Shetty . It was a long distance relationship and still they planned to marry each other. They met Each Other as a common friend. Their first meet was a major disaster and will be remembered by both.

Sudeep saw her profile from her Facebook account and

started a conversation from a fake account. Getting deeper into it Sudeep got to know that Jasmine didn't loved reading books but when they met Sudeep planned to diverge about him being an author and also he was chatting to her from a fake account but before they met Jasmine knew everything and it was not much have a tragedy. All of Sudeep's stories make us believe that true love exists, and all one needs to do is strive for it. Accompanied by his fiancé Jasmine, who Sudeep met on a social media network, he states, "True love exists and I believe that the real essence of love and friendship is fading away these days. The only girl he flirted with on Facebook is now his fiancé. His next book will be about our true love story.

Sudeep was not able to meet Jasmine as he lived in Maharashtra and Jasmine lived in Delhi .Sudeep missed her and also got irritated seeing couples in his college.

Sudeep was also a storyteller what he observed and experienced is what now he used to express to the audience and his fans across the country. He never knew how soon he will gain such big public acclaim.

 Two insecurities whichSudeep shared about taking any creative passion as a job such as writing. First was to convince Indian parents and second was that what to explain the people with whom the boy is going to carry his own life and choose her /him as a life partner.

AJITABHA BOSE

Bringing a drastic change in the writers community Ajitabha has gained fame from the youth. I have been knowing Ajitabha since one year and being with him is an immense pleasure. Everyone wanted to adopt the humble attitude like a Ajitabha

: Since childhood ajitabha was never a Studios boy but was

disciplined. He was drilled towards his work and was obedient. His teachers never used to complain about him in the parents teacher meeting but one line was always fixed " Padhai per ThodaDhyan Dena hoga".
He usually wanted to become a filmmaker since childhood and had a piercing interest in creating videos.

This talent of his was ingrained in his blood as his grandfather and his father was a theater artist.

Ajitabh grew up fighting with his elder brother Arnab in almost every issue as every sibling to. Arnab Bose is his elder brother who is now married and has a cute baby girl Mahi. Love in Jamshedpur was his book where Ajitabha wrote the love story of his brother.
In his school days he was interested in co curricular activities. He participated in various writing competitions. He loves to write essays and letters .Well being a child he was also in a relationship in school days and due to his emigration and long distance relationship it was difficult to handle and Ajitabha too wanted to focus on his career.

There were many financial conditions occurring in his childhood but his parents tried to give a wonderful life to him and his brother .They always said him to make on his life by choosing the right path.
According to him he scored well in his dreadly board exams and completed his school days and also managed to score well in 12th exams. Ajitabha never thought of writing a book but the strongest element was reading, which was in inculcated in him since childhood. He also got up with an interest of writing short stories and within

no time he wrote his first book - "It's my love story " and to show his love towards his inspiration writer SudeepNagarkar he designed the cover page with his and his wife's pic.The
Illustration of the characters was beautifully designed and this is a book filled with emotions ambitions and is fulfilled with dreams and various success and failures , one faces in life.

Once ajitabha got a chance to participate in an anthology. His friends suggested him to Grab this chance to become a published author. The result was out and he was like cloud in nine as was selected for it and he was appreciated by his friends too.
When he was at the age of 18 or 19 he wrote stories and posted it on Facebook. His mentors , relatives and friends appreciated his words and emotions in his story and recommended him to publish a book.

They also referred him to learn about marketing and also the publishing method. Ajitabh has gained Fame across the country due to his concept of inventing Pocket Books. Once while travelling to Jamshedpur he saw a girl reading a novel and she was very disconsolatedso Ajitabha asked "why are you so sad while it is such a beautiful novel by Sudeep sir ?"the girl replied "In this journey I wanted a small book to read but there was no such book available "and an Idea hit Ajitabha's mind and he thought of inventing Pocket Books.

His struggle began because publishing a pocket book was not that simple in India. Many publishers were apprehensive rather they rejected to publish a pocket book. Ajitabha then contacted the CEO of Author's Ink Publication. He believed in himself and never stepped back after so many tries he requested and helped Aniket (CEO)to get into the concept. Within no time his pocket book "In love with Shahrukh Khan "got published and this book had hit the media and the community as he was the first to write a pocket love story, he wanted to meet Shahrukh Khan after he wrote this book. He got the Tweet from Shahrukh Khan himself at 9:15 pm and Ajitabha was rejoicing his happiness. Ajitabha is a great fan of Shahrukh Khan and he is also a big inspiration for Ajitabha. Few days later Ajitabha received a call from the office of Shah Rukh Khan and Shahrukh Khan himself wanted to meet Ajitabha.

The day het met Shahrukh , Ajitabha was in wonders and also was nervous, it was a proud moment for ajitabha and his family and he was feeling self glorified. Not once, not twice ,he met Shahrukh four time and it was a prestigious moment for Ajitabha. He was so nervous while meeting him that he holdedShahrukh's hands . Ajitabha wanted his trend of pocket books to be followed and he wrote three more Pocket Books.

He feels that the formation and evaluation of the story is a greater challenge for him. The story can be written in a page or two but evaluating that is big task. Choice of words, language and grammar is something which has always troubled him. He is still working on them.
He loves writing his imagination and form it a story. His characters in the story are created and thus he starts

enjoying while he writes about them. All his locations are the one which he travelled and thus it becomes easy to portray them in the story.

The next book which he penned was "The pocket love story" which is also available in the leading stores.
The pocket love story is short love story which will make you relive your college days. It revolves around the lives of Ramachandra and Tani, where Ramachandra falls in love with Tani but it isn't the same with her. She doesn't like him at all. Gradually they become friends and enjoy each other's company.
He writes when he wants to write. He doesn't write on daily basis. Writing is an art which needs proper concentration and imagination. He usually writes in a silent place or whenever he is travelling.

He has been a consistent blog writer since 2010. It was in the year 2013, when he published his first story.
The journey so far has been enormous. The love, support and motivation which his well-wishers bestow on him is just beyond his expectations. He will try to live to their expectations and keep entertaining them lifelong.
The fact that The Pocket Love Story holds a national record is helping him creating vibes in the market. Basically his books are very short and thus hardly takes 30 mins of the readers time to complete it. His book doesn't take much space, rather negligible.

It can even easily slip in your back pocket. He always keeps the language very simple so that it can be read by mass. And never the less, his book is full of love, humor and a story which one can easily relate.

Ajitabha since childhood had been a power bank of talent. He is an entrepreneur as he owns his own Studio" Bose documentries Limited" He also started his Ajitabha Publications to give a new Outlook and opportunity to the new authors . Ajitabha has been featured in Limca Book of Records and has been given the title of king of Pocket Books he has more than 20000 followers on social media sites and has been verified on Facebook and Instagram. He also has a keen interest in writing nonfiction books.

His first nonfiction book was the YouTube stars of India which was at a great response from the youtubers and the audience.The youtubers appreciated the words of Ajitabha .His next nonfiction book is on the comedy king Kapil Sharma and his working on this book since 2017.

It is the first book to be written on the journey of the self-made celebrity which will be published under Ajitabha Publishers in collaboration with the Rohan Trust.
The book tells the story of Kapil Sharma from the point when he started his journey. The foreword being written by the legendary superstar, Dharmendra, other celebrities including ArchanaPuran Singh, SonuSood, KikuSharda, SumonaChakravati,   Shruti   Seth,   PranayParmar, SufiyanSiddiquie and many more have also shared their experiences of working with him. His book has been released and he also met Kapil sharma , Akshay kumar and many other celebrities. Everyone appreciared his book and his hardwork.
Behind this easy going persona is a shrewd mind, which

observes everything around him and keeps everyone entertained with his spontaneous humor. Taking all his seven books into consideration, Ajitabha is counted among the most popular and influential authors of the country.

He has been doubtful regarding his voice . He considered his voice to be a Rushy and Harsh and referred to speak less in public places but once he posted a video on his own voice and got a good appreciation from his fans and readers. The confidence was built in him to post more videos and he made reels on Instagram.

Being honest Ajitabha has been very grateful to school and towards his teachers. Ajitabha taught everyone whosoever he found to be determined and to never ignore young talent , always try to accept that talent . At a period of time Ajitabha was not known to everyone but his achievements and works led him to what we are seing now. His mother was given an award from Telegraph on Mother's Day for giving birth to a steel boy of Jamshedpur . On the eve of the Christmas , he never waited for anyone to give him gifts, but he dressed in Santa Claus and distributed clothes, snacks to the needful , he has been helping Students by donating books and he sold his 1 lakh bike to help the people and earn blessing. In one of the interview he referred himself as selfish because he helps people to gain love and blessings, this is a new definition for selfish invented by Ajitabha himself . He has been a role model for many children like me and youngsters too. He has been invited in many shows as a chief guest .

Ajitabha missed his two Ted Talks because due to his busy routine. He has been making 500 + videos and thousand plus posters . We never knew what life becomes after success . Ajitabha had been a great definition for success in life . From a simple family he achieved big . Struggle makes you learn a lot in life . Ajitabha very instrumental towards his work and is also a romantic person. You can connect with him easily on social media sites.

ANSUMAN BHAGAT

Since childhood Ansuman had been an innocent boy. A simple introvert boy who was almost non-existent in his school days, since his personality wasn't something that worked well with socialization. He was someone who would keep to himself and not interact with anyone unless someone else would choose to talk to him. He wasn't someone who held onto an interest on what others thought of him,belonging from a sweet and caring family of Jamshedpur.

From childhood he had a keen interest in playing flute. He has been reading books of Priya Kumar and JK Rowling and is a big fan of them. Ansuman always dreamt and aimed big, he is a person who is very down to earth and also a boy who was interested in co-curricular activities.

Ansuman always wanted to become an actor when he was just 16. The idea of growing into something was new which stood out for Ansuman of his streaming world.He was always alone and focused on studies and he loved to study science and was bored whenever he got usual holidays from school.

He usually tries to bunk school with many excuses with growth. The visualization of Ansuman changed and he focused on his acting career. In class 10 he scored 86% and is marks decrease in class 12th due to his distraction towards acting. He did his Bachelor in mass media over a while he realized that he should also follow his passion towards acting and was stuck upon it. Struggling was a big issue for Ansuman and since childhood he has been a hardworking boy.

As a child he wanted to become a chief minister so that he

can remove all corruptions and make his state dynamically unique but what life made it, was an opportunity for him. He went Mumbai and inclined towards the profession of acting. He has casted in numerous shows as a casting director in Bollywood for more than 3 years and has a good connection with Bollywood stars.

At this point everybody thought that Ansuman has reached his success. He wasn't ordinary when came to childhood interest. When Ansuman started onto his field he was committed towards his dreams he used to imagine about thoughts which strikes his mind and he tries to explore more and work upon it likewise he used to jot down each and every thought which comes to his mind. His friends advised him to turn up the diary very he wrote all the thoughts into a book.

Ansuman was committed towards acting and was new towards publishing platform; he then and now struggled for publishing a book. Soon his book was published worldwide and many VIP's is appreciated his book and now he is on every social media sites with more than 50K followers.

The book got good response from the audience, but his idea of Sustainable mark can only be considered when a person begin to be criticized about their work.I believe not everything can be bought in life,specifically when it comes to hard work and dedication.

One may hold towards his own work which is by Ansuman Had Never backed out from the most little to the most illusive hurdles in his life rather He has fought them through. He believes that if he did hard work and struggles to achieve the key so that the people who hated Ansuman would appreciate him and feel guilty about their words.

Ansuman's father was a transport manager and was very proud of Ansuman about the mark his son was leaving behind via his work. Ansuman was very busy towards his writing career as within few days his book "Your Own Thought"became the best seller which led him to get a public fame.

These causes forced Ansuman to leave his acting career behind. He had always been someone who lived behind the screen but now he was in fame among the youth.

I believe that a worthy, hardworking and real person is blessed to receive a loving and trustworthy audience in his life.Ansuman has lived his ups and downs in his life, but he was also a person struggling for the ticket fare for which he is always grateful to his family.

He has also launched an app for the young talents to give their audition and to host their talent.

Ansuman's work has done wonders to his life and he was nominated in the India book of records and he was the one who got recorded in the book. Ansuman has been a person who inspired the youth and taught how to be determined and also that there is no age limit to move upon and head towards your career.

Being a guy who was an introvert a new environment was a big call for him and tough too
He never fell in love as usually he never got time to continue his relationship. After getting settled he got many proposals though not directly but Ansuman neglected.

Ansuman was an introvert so he usually feels uncomfortable talking to a girl and never loves to share about his love life in any public interview. Additionally he was in love with the infrastructure. During all this while he wondered about writing more books which will inspire the current youth to an extent. He usually writes to motivate most people through which people are actually unable to understand their inner feelings and he writes in very simple Hindi or English, keeping in mind that every person that can be a Chai-wala or a big businessman can read and understand easily.

He hates discrimination and never upholds the caste system which is interviewed by the society. He started his journey writing contents, articles for the local newspaper and got acknowledged about printing.

He has been announced the best inspirational quote writer in India.

The power of letters and style of writing in books make a writer a different from himself who lives in people's mind from generation to generation.

Ansuman believes that readers are more comfortable to read love stories but nevertheless reading motivational book.Often we see authors write books on a single subject but in view to this answer Ansuman inspired people through many topics which he preferred in his book.

Many thoughts are jotted in his books that will make people relax and will energize them to work and also to work on the right path. Now the generation is living only in mobiles and computers by which they are getting away from themselves.

A young author Ansuman is one of the most handsome newcomer to the industry and has a fit body and with impressive personality.

He is a big devotee to Lord Krishna and follows him in every path and decision of his life. He is not addicted towards any bad addiction and he loves to travel and enjoy music.

He also loves nature and loves to plant trees.

He is a fitness freak person love to do Yoga and Gym both.

He always tell people to love themselves as "God help those who help themselves"

In this reel life of social media and Technology people are forgetting the real people.
A person who boasts to be an animal lover annoys Ansuman He wants that every person should understand each other for better Unity.Ansuman is such a person who can teach you to be determined and also he is an influencer who shows you the right track. He tells people that choosing a good career has no age limit. You cans start following your dreams at your wish and let your determination excel it.

Some best quotes written by Ansuman Bhagat

"If you are hungry for success, you are capable of moving on in life"

"Try to recognize your own talent instead of living a pretentious life of imitating others."

"Make yourself able enough to not depend on anyone else."

AJAY KUMAR PANDEY

On the surface Ajay was dearly loved by everyone he met owed to his personality and behaviour.

Ajay was a Opulent guy in his school days and was not much than a Studios guy.

He never thought to be a medallion but always wanted to become instrumental towards his work.

Ajay being brought up in a Hindu family with culture imbibed in him. He belonged from a medial standard family with average circumstances , he was simply bought up from the age 5 to 25.

Since childhood Ajay loved hearing stories and within no time he also ingrained the habit of reading books and writing stories. He was compassionate, tuneful and mellifluous boy with shiny hair and deep black eyes.

Ajay was one of those students who never knew what to achieve in life. He never thought of any goals but was spending his childhood in' bindaas way .

He was fond of reading books of Premchand which comes very easily slitted in Rupees 1 or 50 paise

Ajay did his schooling and however he managed to score quite well.

He also made a girlfriend in school days,Ragini

Ajay was just heading to pursue engineering. He also joined the race, though there were some inpracticablity in his way but somehow he learnt to be a part of the race and also to adjust in it.

To be more focused , joining a coaching institute for IIT exam was not a bad idea Ajay prayed to God at the top of his voice considering God deaf.

He just always centralised on one thing to God to please let him be a IITian and unfortunately god was in confusion .

IIT sounded him IERT so God gifted Ajay with IERT (institute of engineering and rural technology) nevertheless he was not disheartened with IERT but he happily accepted the same.

Ajay went to the college with his father and his father was very proud for Ajay Kumar as he was the first person in the Pandey family to study engineering but Ajay wanted to become a teacher as usual destiny landed to IERT.

Ajay's father was worried of ragging.

The warden explain that ragging has been declared as a criminal offence to there is no issue .

Mr.Pandey had too many questions puzzled in his mind

Mr .Pandey was an ordinary father like others who usually gave Gyan sessions.

In the college he met his friend and also he did jibberish talks and gossips. In the class he met a girl with beautiful attracion.Ajay skipped Ragini and jumped into Bhavna and he was too committed towards her.

Ajay was totally mad in love and was day dreaming

Days passed by and the bond with Bhavana grew stronger
.

Ajay was like a pet of Bhavna and was perfectly in love with her.

Bhavna and Ajay were in a relationship. Bhavna teaches Ajay to live life for others . She makes him live in every matter. Ajay's one thought is always in bold "never focus on the second nameor the surname of the person whom you love and though you never surrender your dreams "An a intercase marriage was a big deal in their families but they did everything to convince their parents . Ajay convinced his parents to let Bhavna be with him. Ajay got inspired from Bhavna to write his first book which got published that was on his real-life . Already there was a futile attempts to meet mainstream publisher and then he found Srishti publishers . His first novel was straightforward chronicle of 10 years long romance of both while eads to death of Bhavna (fictional)after she was striked from dengue.

His first book sold two lakh copies in the world and he became the best selling author in India .

Before he wrote his first book he got into research of romance genre and read books of Chetan Bhagat , SudeepNagarkar, DurjoyDatta and Ravinder Singh . Romance is all about love and emotion. As these kind of novels are close to reality, reader can easily find themselves connected to story and can feel it. The frankness and natural way of storytelling makes it popular and most widely read genre in market.

Ajay was struggling to find publisher while Anisha his friend came up with usual book promotion idea with him. Book launch let to be the best seller .

Anisha also plays a significant role in Ajay's life.

Ajay, Anisha and Arvind and his uncle along with Bhavna and his parents have altogether taught him the importance of love , life and friendship. The main reason to write this novel is to make his wife (Bhavna) memories everlasting. He had tears while holding his first paperback.

This book "You are the best wife" has a beautiful message in his words and emotions expressed has been best experienced by many readers.The book covers the change in how they glance at the world and the way the world looks at them, and how they never give up on their love in face of adversities, until fate reveals its plans after his darling wife left him halfway through their journey. However, Bhavna gives him the power to live on, and carry out his pledge of love as Ajay comes to terms with the prime lesson life has to present. He never thought of writing a book nevermore he had an Idea or interest in writing stories. He is today successful because of his wife Bhavna who made her learn the lesson of life. Ajay wrote a book 'you are the bestfriend' which describes and focuses hardly on Anisha.

She is a believer and challenger in Ajay's lost belief. Ajay's stories are heart touching and one can easily connect with it because it's emotions and pain felt real.

Travelling, trecking and reading takes much of his leisure time . He has explored many countries across the world . He is an Author who writes from heart by keeping the reality intact.

His second book" her last wish" was also inspired by the struggles of and HW patient . Both books were inspired by true elements and hence they are able to portray the greif like no other .Every book of Ajay has their own aspect of transaction . Ajay also grew with big dreams , apart from writing the follows his role model Mother Teresa.

He got aspired to start an Association where he can help people and gain blessing. Ajay is also an inspiration for many readers and writers .I was too inspired from Ajay Sir to write a love story to have experience of love, life and everything. Ajay learnt the art of writing from Buddhadev and Khushwant Singh

ROHIT DAWESAR

Sudden changes happens in our life and this what happened to Rohit.. From a stammer he became a speaker Rohit was an inquisitive boy and was also cunning towards his task. He rarely becomes meally-mouthed towards his work. He was too much focused on school friends ,school and ofcourse his loving Mumma who guided her in every ups and downs and also teaches the way to live life. .Whenever teacher used to call Rohit to read books or to recitate a poem Rohit showed his least interest at that at times. He Used to stammer in his class and the fear was that his friends would poke fun at him .He wanted to hide his habit of stammering so he used to take part in drama and school plays.Rohit thought that it is impossible for him to ameliorate his habit of stammering but he had confidence and the willpower to make impossible things possible

Rohit fagged most of his time with his Jigri friend Birju. Rohit deliberated his homework as boring ,after he completes it he shows his mother ,the words she uses after seeing his homework was like a Padmashree award to Rohit 'Jaokhelo.

 Birju was from a Brahmin family and also was vegetarian.

Birju's mother loved Rohit on each basis .Rohit's mother gave 'Gyan sessions ' to Rohit . She used to tell him that if he doesn't concentrate or intensify towards his studies , he would further wash utensils in some hotel or would run thelas to earn 2 times of roti.

Rohit was an average student and if his mother asks her any question regarding his studies then Rohit would get irritated and angry too.

He was good in dancing and participated in school annual functions. Once in the annual function he did a mistake and the full attention of the audience was on him. Apart from this Rohit takes to maintain his relationship with girlfriend Shrley which is a part of his story line. Rohit always gave a deep and practical insights of love life , career and the hardships which came in between.

Rohit was now a grown up and a mature boy who knows

his rights and wrongs. Rohit went to metShrley's parents because she told she wants to get married with him. Rohit being a handsome and a well qualified boy never got a green signaled from Shirley parents.

Rohit being ambitious and career oriented, he did not notice Shirley's wishes,

 their interest cracked and they were left heartbroken.

Then their love story unfolds in typical Indian society as Sherley leaves. Rohit just to make his parents happy he focused on his career rather than wedding.

Rohit thought of writing the story because he wanted his storyline to be public with the audience. He always used to drop the idea of writing a book because he thinks that he should write after his retirement. Then his friends and mentors advised him to publish the book and let the book reach the audience. His first book The stupid somebody fortunes his memories about childhood and about being in a relationship .Rohit also described about his friend Birju in the book. This book mainly devotes true friendship, love and happiness .Rohit being a child wanted to become a spiderman when he used to think about his aims he also wanted to become an astronaut or sometimes an actor... when he was in class 10 he thought to be an actor but stammering was a dense problem of Rohit.

Rohit first book was a great response from the readers. The cover page of the book indicates a very hearty and accurate message . After he wrote his first book an ideas striked his mind that he should succeed over his Passion of writing and he wrote his second book after a period of one year.Rohit also writes and posts nanotales , short stories and one – liners on social media which receives love from his readers all over the globe and Rohit has gained more than 20,000 followers on social media. The story which Rohit wrote for Building his readership when he began writing was titled "Walk on a Goa beach "(later the same story was converted as a full-fledged book which is now his latest novel"No matter what").

His second book No matter what was a carefully crafted love story that happens between two people who take care of every nuisance in the relationship, nurture it and grow it. It was such a honest intense and also a story blended with responsibilities and conduct.

 Love stories are those stories that a built like every story they have a beginning they have a drama in it and they have a ending. Isn't it ?Rohit received comments that he must start writing quite often. Rohit was an avid reader and people would have found his thought process and understanding about life and thought process little attractive.

His words create a magic in our hearts .He owns a coaching institute for engineering students where he used to inspire them and also he has posted some professional teachers to teach the students.

He is the co-founder of an restaurant 'The urban Gumti'.

Rohit always had a Passion of speaking and he opts to become a motivational speaker and therefore he does follow it.

Whenever he used to think about being the speaker he makes a sad face for the reason that he stammers a lot.

Once his friends told him and some teased about his

stammering and Rohit got committed towards speaking and joined classes, practiced and he is now a well classified, motivational speaker.

Rohit used to take masterclass which are reviewed by many people . He taught students engineering and also teaches them the main motive of life.

Rohit used to take training classes - Entrepreneurship and always loved to spread knowledge but there was only one thing in his life which always made in anxious was his stammering.

Inlife everybody have a story and they think that it is interesting or charimastic one which they think is the best and Rohit thought the same but he was encouraged to write book at the same point of the time and he completed writing his book, but he found difficulty for finding a publisher for his work.

Amazing fact was that after he published his Novel which became the best seller among the Bollywood stars and also the public loved it a lot.Rohit felt really good beyond explanation.

The tag also bought also bought with it a responsibility to strive and become better with each book.Rohit's current publisher is quite helpful and they share the same goal to make the book successful. They also help to make the book reach to the right target.

Rohit was also a champion in tennis and while pursuing his class 12 board exams he won the Tennis Championship in his state and that was a proud moment for Rohit and his family

Rohit's mother never appreciated him ,but this time she was too happy for Rohit, and his father was also cherished . Usually nobody used to praise Rohit as his sister was a district topper and she was always praised by his teacher and also by his parents

His sister is now married and lives with her husband in greater Noida . Recently she was blessed with a baby girl and Rohit with beautiful Niece.

Rohit believes that ideas are like the air we breathe, they are everywhere.

Rohit reads the reviews of his book and feels happy when he reads good reviews and feels angry when he comes across any negative review. The reviews are negative because they just want to target him,and these reviews were the ones which affected him badly in his initial days.He used to get angry and sad but later he concludes that they haven't even actually read the book . Perhaps they have some other Agenda.

Rohit sends lots of love to the readers.............

STUTI CHANGLE

An Endearing girl , hailing from a small town of Indore came up with a new concept and also with a new passion. Born on 11th September 1992 at Christian Missionary Hospital in Tilda near Raipur, she grew up in a middle class family. Her father Was a Banker , employed in State Bank of India and her mother worked in a government job as a school teacher.She was raised in various cities across India due to her father's job that demanded relocation every few years. Moving to a new city every few years contributed to her extroverted personality and love for travel. Stuti also has a younger brother, Swapnil.

Stuti's love for books dates back to her school years where she would often spend time reading fiction and geography in the library. While her friends spent time with their boyfriends, Stuti moved to the library. She was a nerd while growing up and bullied for her dark complexion, hairy skin, big teeth, braces and wearing heavy spectacles. She mostly confided in books. Nancy Drew, Famous Five, Sidney Sheldon, Stephanie Meyer, Peter Pan were some of her favourite reads as a teenager. It was only after she read 'The White Tiger' by AravindAdiga, 'Fight Club' by Chuck Palahnuik and 'Into the Wild' by Jon Krakauer that she felt thoroughly motivated to write a book someday.

When she was 2, she wanted to be an astronaut.

When she was 4, she wanted to be a doctor.

When she was 8, she wanted to be a teacher.

Whe she was 12, she wanted to be a writer.

But when she was 16, she was sitting with a bunch of bright students in an IIT-JEE coaching class. While these students were going to make their parents and the country proud, she had no idea where her life was going to take her.

Now, let's take a pause, you might wonder – What went wrong?

She wanted to be an astronaut because the stars would fascinate her.

She wanted to be a doctor because it was the 'in' thing to

do back in time.

She wanted to be a teacher because her mom is a teacher and she loves the fact that her mother added values to others and got immense love and respect in return. However, she wanted to be a writer because she did not have any specific reason. She just loved writing and words came naturally to her. When she was 12, she wrote a poem, a day before the math exam as it rained heavily. Everyone appreciated her capacity to translate emotions into words. She also got picked by a local English Newspaper. The joy of being published was immense.

Since childhood she reported her 10x version of a story. People would often call her a 'nautanki'. She takes it to her heart and cried on most of the days, until one day she realized that it was actually a God's gift and her perspective on anything and everything was so unique. Moreover, she was passionate about telling stories. What people said or thought of her ceased to matter anymore.

Herparents weren't supportive and she doesn't blame it on them. People, who love you, actually want you to have a stable life and a secured future. That's the way society has run for a very long time. But it had ceased to have any effect on her. She decided to embrace the struggle because she was sure of achieving her dreams someday.

Stuti was a bright student with a 90+ academic record throughout. She was recognised in the top 10 students upon leaving higher secondary school in 2010. She wanted to pursue English Literature but did not find support from her family. Stuti graduated with a BE degree in Computer Science and Engineering from SVITS, Indore in 2014. She was offered with TCS Hyderabad on campus but chose to go for further education. Stuti scored 94 percentile in CAT and then went on to do an MBA in Marketing from the prestigious International Management Institute, New Delhi and post-graduated in 2016.

Stuti briefly worked with corporates like HSBC and Coffee Day Beverages in Pune and Mumbai respectively before taking the plunge in 2016 after watching the film 'Fight Club' for the 8th time. Her husband Kushal was her then-boyfriend working on his startup. He encouraged her to quit the rat race and work passionately for her long lost dream of becoming a published author. She still feels she is blessed to have a mentor like him.

Luckily,her friend turned husband , is a successful entrepreneur and he's been like a mentor since day one. She has so much to learn from him and he never steps back from sharing his wisdom.

Her book You live only once has a great impact on readers.The author weaves magic with her words, as the thoughts of Alara and Ricky are pure bliss; their thoughts and emotions are compelling. The quotes at the start of each chapter are interesting; Aarva's standup acts though impressive could have been better presented. Pick this one for an enigmatic story that is coming-of-age filled with music, fun, love and much more. You live only once is an experience that every reader should drown in at least once.

In 2018, she started a coffee table book venture with her friend but they later had to shut it down as the Indian companies in Gurgaon were not ready to spend on coffee table books and felt that the product was an unnecessary luxury.

In 2019, she made her TV debut as she hosted the series 'KarKeDikhayenge.' She was approached by one of her mentors, AmitSinghal, who felt that she could pull off the role with ease as she's talented at speaking effortlessly. The entire TV Series broadcasted every week on Hindi Khabar Channel, Jio Network and Talentopedia platform.

Through these years, she decided not to give up on her dream of becoming a successful author and persevered to build a vibrant community of readers & followers on social media that she addresses as #SCFamily. She interacted with her community and discussed her books, ideas, travel, life, dreams, startups, love and much more.

Stuti loves to dance. It keeps her spirits up and her body in shape. She has been trained as a classical Kathak dancer by her mother who has been awarded by Raj Kapoor and is an exceptional dancer. Stuti is an avid reader. She read more fiction while growing up. On the contrary, she mostly reads non-fiction titles now. Some of her favourite writers are AravindAdiga, Chuck Palahnuik, Paolo Coelho, Haruki Murakami, Premchand, NidaFazli, Rumi, Italo Calvino, JJ Abrams, Mitch Albom, Sidney Sheldon, JK Rowling and Ruskin Bond.

Stuti loves to sing and recite. She could memorise more than 400 nursery rhymes as a three-year-old. She still can memorise most of the songs she listens to! She credits the overnight success of her second book to the years of consistent hard work and learning from every failure that came her way after quitting her corporate career. She campaigned on her own for three years – travelled to every corner of India, built a social media presence, packed and dispatched books to customers, and spent sleepless nights in a row. Her in-laws, new family, also helped her with managing book operations as she turned her home into a warehouse post marriage.tuti has partnered with the NGO

Voice of Slum and helps them raise funds through various initiatives. Her second book 'You Only Live Once?' was launched by children from Voice of Slum. Women empowerment, child education & welfare and environment conservation are a few issues very close to her heart.

ADITYA NIGHOT

We cannot deny to the fact that talent is uncountable .
Being a perfect boy came along with divergence of a
seculed personality .Aditya believed in his parents and was
the winsome and dearest of his parents. Aditya was nor a
funny kid but was weiry. His childhood was never

struggling nor his adulthood. I belong from upper middle class family where is father was an officer of Government of Maharashtra and his mother was M.science teacher as profession. He got inspired to read and write from his valiant grandpa who was an army officer and served as the captain of Indian Army. Referring to Aditya no one can beat the efforts he has put behind publishing is book . He has now gained 17000 plus followers on social media and has a public Fame. The idea of growing onto something comprehensive and what stood out for Aditya in a very initial age of his andous work. Aditya was obsessed about science in his childhood and was dedicated towards reading and writing. He did a lot of experiments which led him to get scolded but he never heard backed confidence.

Class 10 was a big demo for him as he was going to be seated in board exams and for which he did Fortune hard work. He scored well but he expected more. Aditya was a introvert and a Studios boy you never used to talk or love to share his inner-case feelings to anyone if he didn't finds the satisfied person.

He has never been mealymouthed towards his studies or any task provided to him. He always had an interest in plant and animals referring to science and wished to excel in them either. He never wanted to be a charming star of school rather also not being a dump. Sitting at a corner and getting stuck with books and then he would not interact with anyone if he didn't find any comfort level . Aditya loves to read crime fiction as it takes him altogether to a different world zone . He was able to think like a criminal and his brain cells gets stimulated. Aditya develops and idea of coming up with a new story when he closes his eyes, turns on some music and start living characters in the book.

His brain and heart co-ordinate with emotions ,the characters experiences and pens down into words.

He just discovered the writer all of a sudden in himself . He never planned to be a writer and never even dreamt of writing a book. He started writing at the age of 17 as he realised that his story should reach the audience.

The audience should read and share their feelings and that's all how it began with him. Aditya was ragged down while finding a publisher for him . Aditya also had a keen interest in photography and also he did a short course from YatinDandekha photography. Over a period of time when he wrote his story and people crosswise country got inspired from Aditya and his book was found to be in Trend.

He got selected for the best romance novel in India and initially it was a merry ride when it came up to reviews Aditya has been giving interviews in many platforms.

 He has been a hardworking child as he was pursuing MBBS and was writing too. Aditya was a medical aspirant and he never got time to follow his passion .

Before the thought of writing he did a lot of exploration of the genre . He read number of books to know more about it, he wrote the book within three months . He didn't got time to write in the morning or in the evening but he used to write after midnight.

Everybody has a fear in their life and Aditya was also one of them. Whenever there is a moment , when he is in terror and also helpless then he would be panic.

 His parents are not just supporting on their moral compass but gave him a open arm whenever needed.

They Never Backed Down to any of their decisions of

life.

Aditya's book within no time received initial as well as public acclaim and helped Aditya sell more than 20000 copies in a month.

Aditya's debut novel U n Me . . . It's Complicated!!! was originally written as a hobby with limited copies printed for friends, family and a few readers. But the positive reviews he received encouraged him to write another novel. His book Until Love Sets Us Apart, previously titled In the Blink of an Eye, won the "Best Romance Book of the Year" Award and has inspired him to write more. He is currently working on his next novel.

Until Love sets us apart is an emotional love story, but unlike any other normal love story, this story has depth, it will take you on an emotional spin and yet you won't feel exhausted. It will make you smile, it will make you cry, and it will also define true love. Overall, it's definitely a book drenched in love and romance and must be read if you love this genre.

His books are on the way to be displayed on the T.v screen and Aditya wants his favourite actors Adityaroykapoor and Shraddhakapoor to play this significant role.

Aditya when he was a child was in love but in his growing years he realise that childhood love is no more but stupidity. He did an online dating few years back when he was just 22 and that went bad because Aditya was not interested in an online dating and wanted a long term relationship .

Whenever an idea strikes his mind he would love to Pen it down without any second thought. If he wouldn't be a doctor then he wished to be in film ethics. Aditya's narration is very powerful. His narration is at a very dynamic point of view and also in a very exclusive and simple English.

His words keeps readers hooked. Aditya feels that he can connect to youth's emotion and Express through his books . His writing has been proved as a a book for the audience . He as a doctor has also helped covid patients in this Complex time for which he has been appreciated by many.

He has Experienced many moments in his life but one was a big moment which he shared with us. When he received an email from one of his readers that he saved his life as he was going to commit suicide and he read his book and got motivated to come out of depression , it was a heart melting moment for everyone.

We always wanted to give a message to his readers to believe in yourself and never let negativity affect your career as you are blessed to be able to achieve the same.

Aditya being such a sweet boy is happily married with a beautiful girl and they are happily blessed.

HIMANSHU RAI

Being from a small town of Madhya Pradesh, Himanshu came up with writing stories . Himanshu showed least interest in reading but as he grew up , his interest in writing was built . In childhood he used gather paper and wrote novels of 10 pages and used to to stick them. He used cardboard to make cover pages ,which he found to be creative. Giving more attention and importance to drama and plays , Himanshu won many prizes which was a proud moment for him being a small kid.

Himanshu did his schooling at Saint Joseph School and till class 6 he was little furnished towards studies but was not a topper rather he was a average student.

He scored between 70% which his father didn't expected from him. A sudden turn came up in a studies when he was in class seven and he met an major accident due to which his hand got fractured and he was suffering from severe pain. He was unable to attend any of the exam but however he was promoted to class 8 with average grades and soon in the month of April, he recovered. After he recovered , he was committed towards his studies and was oriented towards it. Statingly however he managed to score good till class 10.

An incident took place in his life which became a moment for him. Getting to the past when Himanshu was in class 10. He was heading towards his school and before he goes to school he visits his friend's apartment. His friend lived in the second floor and in the ground floor there was a herd of cows standing. Himanshuenvicted the cows and went to his friend's house but he didn't noticed that one of the cows has urinated in the ground floor which has entered one of the houses. While they were chit chatting and were getting ready to head back to school one man came and knocked the door. Himanshu's friend father opened the door and the man yelled and told that Himanshu has urinated in his house. His father was astound and then he denied telling "how can he do this?

he belongs from a good family and is a grown up boy." The man was not at all listening to them and showed the urine. Suddenly Himanshu's friends father started laughing and exclaimed that Himanshu has not done this. He told that this is half a bucket of urine and it is impossible for a human being to do this. Himanshu then told that the cows which were standing here, they must have done this but the man was still not ready to trust them.The society members made him apprehend towards the situation.

Himanshu didn't skipped the moment and wanted to take revenge as the man made him feel guilty in front of everyone.

One day Himanshu was standing in his balcony and was looking through a new version of magazine and instantaneously he saw the same man who blamed him. The man

came to pick her daughter from her tuitions.

Himanshu saw cow's dung near the scooter and he was just finding the right

time to take revenge.He came downstairs and started shouting that this man

has done his dung near the scooter.The man was continuous denying .

Himanshu's father scolded him and told " Are u blind ? Can't you see that this is a cow dung?".Himanshu exclaimed that if this mam can blame me telling cow's urine as mine they why can't I tell cow's dung as his.Himanshu was scolded but he was satisfied........

Himanshu used to listen poetry and also his father used to translate it which assisted Himanshu to answer easily in his exams. Innocence was the essence of his childhood as being born in a joint well do family where he never felt alone and was always in a Jolly mood. In class 12 he won the voting of Health and Finance Minister of the school and he was busy in that meticulous work . Him being super excited to complete his tasks and attend plays and drama , he was unable to concentrate in his studies and believed that he will score good , rather we can say that he was overconfident.

The bad score is scored was the reason for his depression. From the day he scored bad, he got systematic towards his studies and was always punctual towards his work. Himanshu's mind keeps on rotating on each and every task and he instills every hobby within him. He is in love with all his books he writes. You got to learn a lot from his grandfather BB Rai who was the freedom fighter , an active politician and also was a doctor. Himanshu used to have a theatre group in which they used to write stories for their plays and then they performed in front of their elders. His grandfather used to appreciate him by giving him one banana each on their performance. I would describe Himanshu in one word then I should say him into 'Enthusiastic '

His career of writing started when he was in Jabalpur ,where he was attending his friend's wedding and it's the City from where he completed his engineering.. nostalgic feeling of those days hold Himanshu to Pen down his best seller book "My mute girlfriend".

Himanshu never follows one genre as whatever comes in his mind he used to pen it down. He also wrote 'Rhythm Roger' which is a science fiction and is all divergent from a Romance novel.

Himanshu's writing style is simple and lucid. The narration had the power to capture its readers . His books are definitely unpuldownable. Himanshu is a Telecom professional with passion of storytelling. Telecom and imagination can never be the part and parcel of the same coin. But young author, HimanshuRai, differs. He is a successful telecom professional and now a writer who connects the two impossible joints of telecom and literature using his impeccable imaginary vision and writing skills. He never used to get time for writing so he used to write after midnight and with a tranquil mind. He is married and also he is blessed with a smart boy who loves to create videos.

Himanshu is one of the author who never backed down his confidence . There are also some more books to come up and Himanshu is trying hard to work upon them as he wanted his book to touch Reader's heart .

DEVANSHI SHARMA

Entering the writer's community was not that easy for Devanshi. She started her journey from being a Straightforward and a simple girl . She is a chatter box till now and makes friend easily and ofcourse she starts chatting with them if she finds him/her suitable and comfortable. She is a person who dissolves gently with people but once she does, she makes friend for lifetime. For her ,Literature means world. Having been a student of English Literature herself, She feels that literature is one subject that covers all layers of human behavior and society. So, when you want to know everything about human beings, you refer to literature.

An observer by nature, a writer by choice and a storyteller by passion – Devanshi is a combination of these.

She loves reading Indian authors, naming a few they are, Ruskin Bond for the reason that how he defines mountains, no one else can. Another writer she loves is ManjuKapoor for her realistic and gray characters.She is a foodie and tries different haute cuisines. Devanshi is always curious about knowing and experimenting. Devanshi loves eating but she never tried cooking stuffs nor she helped her mom in cooking . Her mother generally used to scold her for not learning cooking. Devanshi within her growing years, learnt to cook Maggie and also tried to cook something new.Devanshi only loved to cook up stories rather than cooking food.

Her writing journey started when she was reading in class 9. Once her mother was gifted a laptop and Devanshiwas eccentric to work on the laptop.She started writing an article and after a month she realized that, this article has turned up too long. So she thought to turn up the story into a book and that how's she began her writing.

Her parents were unknown about the fact that Devanshi has applied for publishing her book.

Her parents were always supportive towards her and they

always wanted a finest and a foremost result from Devanshi. She was an average student till class 10 and managed to score almost well. She loved playing with the dolls, usually which every girl does.

After she came up with her first book when she was reading up on for the 12th board exams, she gained fame in her school and people started appreciating her towards her industrious work. Her first book gave her the confidence to come up with more books. Devanshi being fascinated about writing, she wrote 5 books which didn't affect her career.

Her latest novel ' I think I am in love' published by Shristi publishers was in sale among the youth and it crossed 10,000 copies . She was glad seeing her book to become the bestseller and she was like cloud in nine.A major part of the book is taken up by the initial marriage sequences and few other moments spent by the lead characters, with each of them expressing their point of views about the other person. The second half has more of the story happening, as the first half tries to build the main characters and their back story.

Devanshi was loved by everyone she met and greet for her humble and noble work. She never tries to adopt any bad features in herself. Her one line is always amazing "Readers make writers" which is a veracity.Devanshi started up with an initiative called "Mithaas" which was to help needful children in fulfilling their needs. Devanshi started this initiative when she was in class 11. They used to collect Rs 10 every week and also they conducted workshops for helping the students by providing them soft boards , chart papers and many other stuffs.

Her childhood was spent more in reading and writing. While her friends were having fun,Devanshi used to think of stories and presupposed of characters.

There were carnivals held in school an Devanshi was in class 10th. Actually she was happy seeing the stall set up and everything they have done as a team with six friends. There team work was successful. She choosed to take up Humanities for her further studies.

Her style of writing is very different as she can't take up one character for a very long period of time. Her story can be related to our own life and it seems to be realistic. She is 25 now and she has come up to the industry with five blockbuster books and there are also more to come up.

The perspective of the readers and the reviews they put up means a lot for Devanshi as earlier she told that "Reader makes writer". She always respects the reviews. If she comes across any negative reviews she tries to makes the things right.

Neatness is a common remark Devanshi got as she used to be responsible towards the task, she is offered and also her things are well-ordered and skilful. She also loves to travel and while travelling also she is fond of writing. Her book usually depicts love, friendship, family time and many more aspects of life. Her each book shares the idea of chasing the dreams and fulfilling them. Dreams are very loyal to us as they will never betray you . Her book "i think i am in love" is also transfigured in Hindi language.

Coming up with five books was not easy and Devanshi has also reached a fairly success. Imagination and love for stories are the most valuable in her journey . Even as a kid,she loved making up stories and narrating them, she is doing the same, the only difference is that now, they are more realistic!

Her family is the first priority in her life, after which comes writing and then the list concludes. So, that's writing in her life right now. She think that each person and each character is shaped individualistically and therefore, comparing two individuals is not something she usually prefers. So, she would say resemble to Devanshi!.

She always used to tell the aspiring writers "I know writing is a journey in itself, with waves of ups and downs but just stick to your story and make it happen, trust me after all the waves, you will never regret the amount of work, effort and emotions that you've put in your work! On that note, Keep writing!"